Pirates

C O N T E N T S

Collins*Children'sBooks*

Enter the Pirate

You're probably familiar with the likes of this swashbuckling rogue, but did you know that pirates first took to the seas in ancient times?

PIRATE PEDIGREE

Just how long ago did pirates bring dread to the Med?

1 2000BC Phoenician pirates.
2 600BC Greek sea raiders.
3 100BC Roman rogues.

A CAUTIONARY TALE

When a band of pirates held the Greek god Dionysus to ransom, legend has it that he turned them all into dolphins and threw them into the water as a warning to other would-be sea robbers.

Caesar seized

In 75BC Julius Caesar was kidnapped by pirates. A huge ransom was paid for his release but the pirates got their just desserts when Caesar's army tracked them down and slaughtered them. Eight years later, the Roman general, Pompey, led a campaign to stamp out piracy: he rounded up 30,000 men and 1,700 ships in the Mediterranean.

Violent Vikings

From AD800 Vikings pillaged Europe's shores, often snatching gold and silver loot from defenceless monasteries.

Monkey business

In the 13th century a French monk-turned-pirate called Eustace terrorised the Channel. It was said he was in league with the Devil and could make his ship invisible.

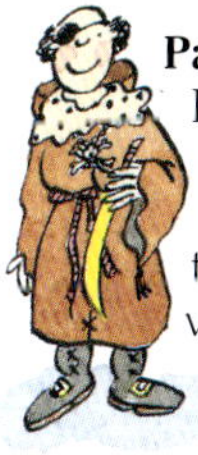

Pay and go away

In AD865 the Saxon king of England paid Viking raiders a bribe to stop them plundering coastal villages. It was called 'Danegeld' and was collected as a tax from local people.

ALIAS PIRATE

Don't be deceived. You'll meet all kinds of sea robbers in this book. Their names may be different but their dastardly deeds are not!

- Corsairs prowled the Mediterranean Sea.
- Buccaneers sailed the Caribbean Sea, the Atlantic or the Indian Ocean.
- Privateers had a licence from their governments to attack ships belonging to enemy countries.

Cunning Corsairs

The Mediterranean was a dangerous place in the days when Muslim and Christian corsairs battled out their religious differences.

CORSAIR GALLEY

Turning Turk
Christian captives of Muslim corsairs faced a life of hard labour. One way to escape this fate was to 'turn Turk' which meant swapping sides and adopting the Muslim faith.

GALLEY FACTS

With the rowing power of 300 oarsmen, a galley could speed towards its target and immobilise the enemy ship with its battering ram. Galley slaves were chained together, six to an oar, and forced to row in time to a drumbeat. If they flagged, they were flogged.

Fighting talk

Christian corsairs carried razor-sharp rapiers into battle and often wore metal helmets and breastplates. The favoured Muslim blade was the curved nimcha that could cut cleanly through Christian necks.

Blood brothers

The Barbarossa brothers were the most feared Muslim corsairs of their day. After many violent clashes with crusader knights and Spanish soldiers, Aruj Barbarossa was killed in 1518. Khair-ed-din vowed to avenge his older brother's death and went on to become the ruler of Algiers.

Pirates of the East

It was a hazardous trip sailing from the Orient to the West with tempting cargoes of silk, spices, gemstones and pearls. In the 16th century buccaneers and privateers from the Caribbean headed east to compete with Indian and Chinese pirates for a share of the plunder.

Heads you lose
Human heads were highly prized trophies brought back after a raid by Chinese pirates. The razor-sharp dao sword could slice cleanly through flesh and bone, while the blowpipe fired a poison-tipped dart with deadly results.

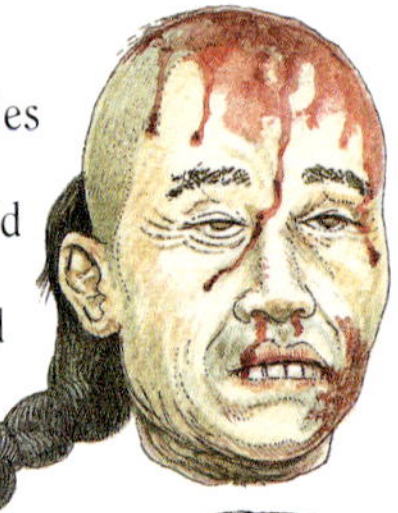

Blood money
There's nothing like a nasty threat to get you what you want. Chinese pirates took hostages and issued ransom notes to extort huge sums of money from rich merchants.

SEA SICK

Indian pirates sometimes forced their captives to drink a foul cocktail of ground tamarind root and sea water and then inspected the vomit in case the desperate hostages had swallowed any pearls or jewels.

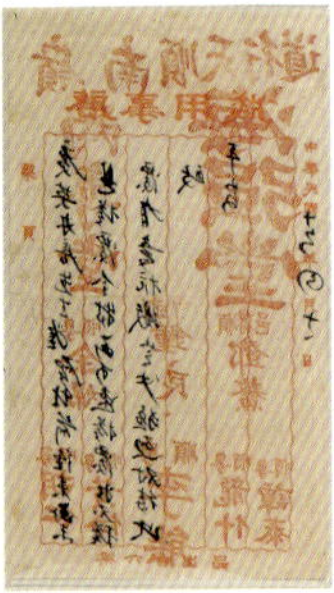

RANSOM NOTE

Junks and dhows

When Chinese pirates captured a trading junk they turned it into a fast, sturdy fighting vessel armed with up to 15 cannons. In the Indian Ocean, many pirates favoured the traditional dhow for chasing swiftly after a merchant ship.

The swampy coastline along the narrow Strait of Malacca, with its coves and creeks, was the perfect hide-out for pirates and a very risky stretch of water for trading ships.

Beware the bogeyman

The Bugi pirates attacked shipping in the Far East. European sailors dreaded any encounter with these sea robbers and their name even gave rise to the English word 'bogeyman', meaning a terrifying monster.

An eastern Jolly Roger?
This manic-looking character is actually T'ien Hou, an oriental goddess that was chosen by a band of 19th-century Chinese pirates to decorate their flag. The bats that you can see down the side were good luck symbols.

The Golden Age of Piracy

When Spanish colonists rushed to the Americas in search of great riches, their plunder began attracting the attention of privateers and buccaneers. The Spanish Main soon became the best hunting ground in the history of piracy!

Pirate or privateer?
Other European rulers didn't just sit back as Spain looted the New World. They authorised daring sailors to hijack the Spanish treasure ships. Queen Elizabeth's most determined privateer was Francis Drake.

Spanish revenge
King Philip II of Spain got so fed up with Drake's raids that in 1588 he sent a convoy of 130 ships, known as the Armada, to invade England... but it was defeated by the English fleet.

The French buccaneer, Francis L'Ollonais, was notorious for his savagery. On one occasion, he ripped out the heart of a Spanish victim, chewed it and then stuffed it into the mouth of another. Yuck!

BAR-B-Q!

Buccaneers learned how to fend for themselves on Caribbean islands. They usually reeked of the smoked meat they cooked over an open fire or 'boucan'. In fact, that's how they got their name!

Hideaway life
When they weren't at sea, the first buccaneers lived as outlaws on remote Caribbean islands. They hunted wild pigs and sold the meat and hides to passing ships.

End of an era
The British Navy launched its ultimate fighting vessel in the battle against piracy in the 18th century. The 'man of war' could out-gun even the most ferociously armed pirate ship.

Shiver Me Timbers

Pirates were pretty particular about the ships they captured. Their villainous vessels had to be fast, seaworthy and well-armed. A firm favourite was the small but speedy two-masted schooner.

GET KNOTTED!

Pirates took pride in their rigging and after a storm or battle they worked for hours splicing and mending the torn ropes. Any pirate worth his salt would know how to tie a reef knot (good for securing rolled-up sails), a half-hitch and a cat's paw (ideal for attaching rope to a hook).

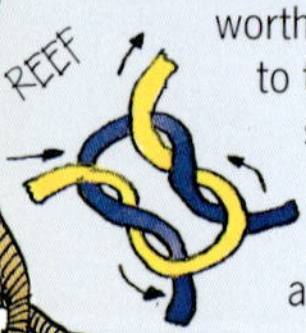

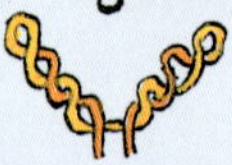

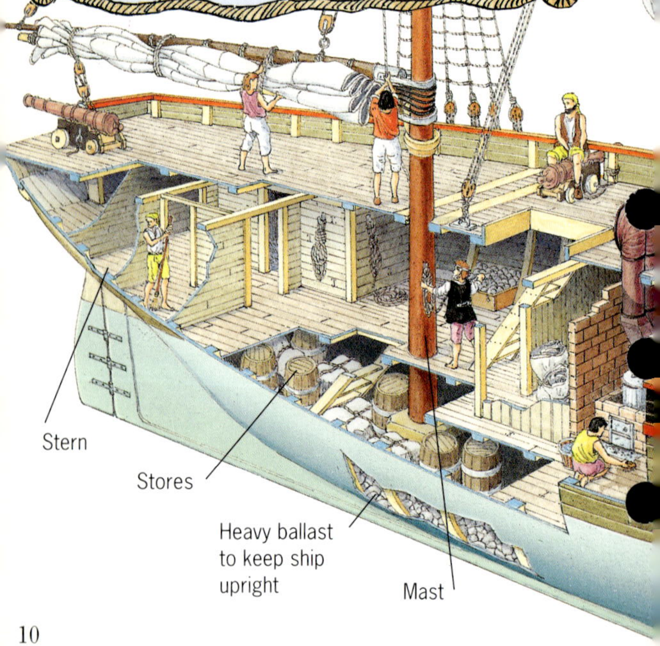

Pirate DIY

A ship was slowed down by the build-up of barnacles and weeds on its hull. So every few months pirates had to beach their ship in a secluded bay, heave the vessel on to its side, and use sharp tools to scrape off the unwanted growth.

Crowded!

Pirate crews were huge (more than 200 men). Large numbers were a must for hand-to-hand combat and manning the guns, but made life on board rather cramped!

JOLLY ROGERS

The terrifying trademark of the skull and crossbones flag would strike fear into the heart of anyone who saw it. Pirate captains each had their own deadly designs.

Jack Rackam's flag

Christopher Moody's flag

Blackbeard's flag

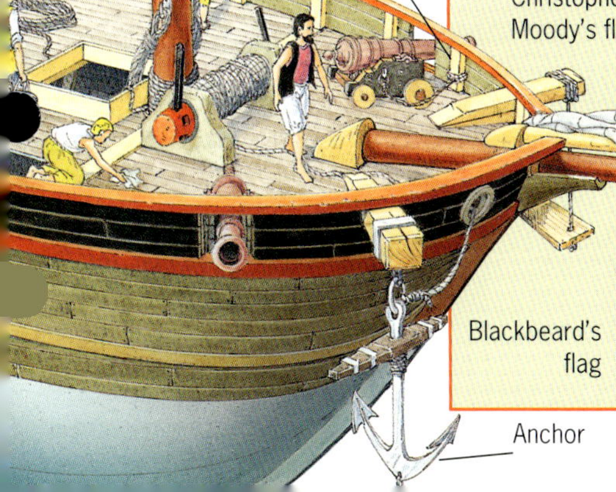

Villainous Voyages

Sailing the high seas was a risky business in the days before accurate methods of navigation. Pirates had to rely on good luck and good weather, and hope that their navigators were sober!

TOOLS OF THE TRADE

Pirate navigational tools were usually stolen! The astrolabe helped sailors judge where a ship was in a north–south direction (latitude).

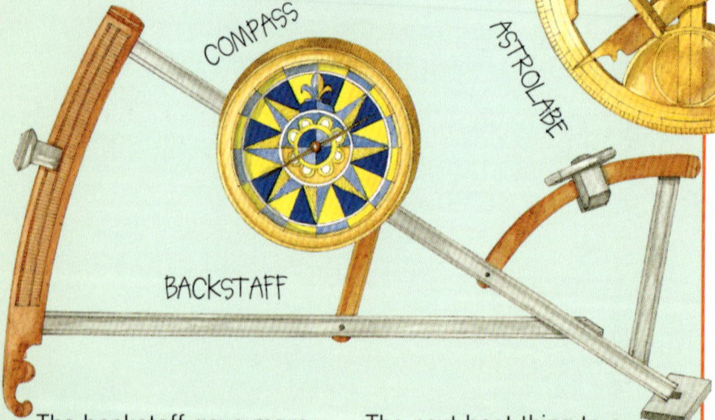

The backstaff gave more accurate latitude readings. But it was not until 1760 that navigators could work out their position in an east–west direction (longitude).

The next best thing to a stolen compass was to get hold of a lump of lodestone. Stroking a needle with this magnetic rock would make a rough and ready compass.

Chart or art?

Beautifully drawn sea charts, collected together in books called 'waggoners', were much sought after by pirates. Although lovely to look at, these charts were often wildly inaccurate. The buccaneer William Dampier reckoned that his stolen charts over estimated the width of the Atlantic by 600 nautical miles!

Bring 'em near!
From the crow's nest (at the top of the main mast) a pirate on telescope duty had the vital job of looking out for hidden coves or spying an unsuspecting victim vessel.

TALES OF THE UNEXPECTED

The crew could be just as unpredictable as the weather! If a captain was unpopular with his men, he could find himself the target of a bloodthirsty mutiny.

At the rate of knots
A ship's speed was measured in knots. A knotted rope was let out into the water. The number of knots that were drawn off the reel (while a 28-second sand-glass emptied itself) gave the ship's speed.

Shipwrecked
Pirate ships on the Spanish Main had to be prepared to ride out storms at sea. But if a boat was sailing close to the shore, high winds and enormous waves could drive it against the rocks. On the other hand, if there was no wind, being 'becalmed' on the open ocean, while food stocks rapidly ran out, was a fate worse than death.

It's a Sea Dog's Life

When pirates weren't engaged in swashbuckling action, life at sea was routine and grim. Ships were dark, filthy and always stank of bilge water and mildewed sails. The food was revolting, your clothes were damp and flea-ridden and at night you were kept awake by rats scratching or the groaning of sick and wounded men.

VITTALS 'N' GROG

Hard tack biscuits were doled out on a daily basis. They were made of just flour and water and came in two flavours: plain or ready-weevilled! Meat and fish were a rare luxury and had to be smothered in salt to stop them going off. Occasionally one of the scrawny goats that wandered about below deck would be killed to make an evil-smelling stew and, for a real treat, there could even be fresh turtle on the menu. When food supplies ran out, a little more culinary imagination was required. In 1670 Captain Morgan's half-starved crew dined on roasted leather satchels! Without any fresh water, pirates washed everything down with brandy, rum or beer.

The last resort

In cases of severe starvation, there are reports of dying crew members being sacrificed to feed the others.

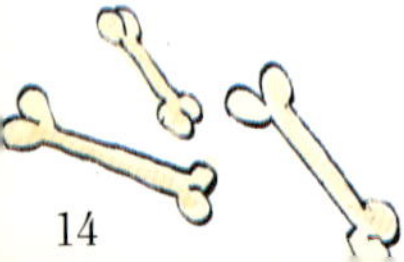

Water-loo!

When a pirate needed to relieve himself he had to go to the bow of the ship and climb down on to a wooden seat with a hole in it.

Hammocks were first used on ships in the 16th century.

Health hazards

Any sea dog would be lucky to escape disease, seasickness, scurvy (from a lack of fresh fruit) or food poisoning. Pirates ran the added risk of being wounded in battle. If amputation was necessary, the patient (preferably blind drunk) was held down while the surgeon hacked off the limb. The raw stump was then sealed with tar.

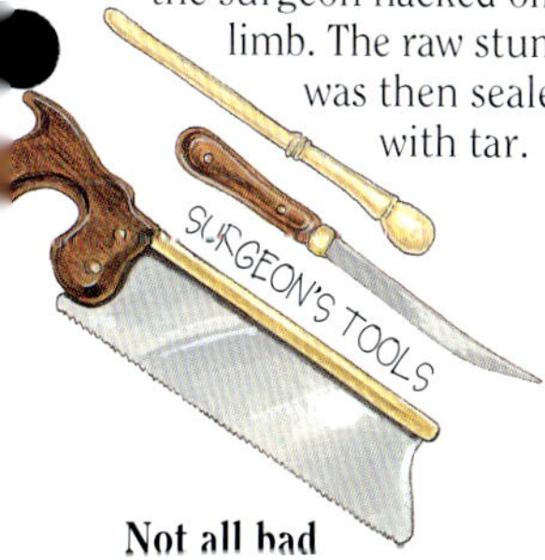

PERFECT PETS

An exotic pet could relieve the boredom of being on board. Pirates preferred parrots (as they could be taught to speak) or monkeys (as they could learn to do tricks).

Not all bad

After a hard day's slog, pirates liked nothing better than to relax on deck: drinking, dancing to the strains of a fiddle, chewing tobacco (smoking was a fire risk), telling yarns and enjoying a rowdy game of dice or cards.

Haunts and Habits

What did it take to be the perfect pirate? You had to look the part, agree to the tough terms and conditions and still be game for a laugh when you went off duty.

Pirate particulars
After months of keeping their balance on a heaving deck, pirates could be spotted by their swaying gait when they came ashore. And you'd need a pirate phrase-book to understand their sea-dog slang.

Pirates served under a captain (1) and usually appointed a first mate (2), surgeon (3) and carpenter (4). The rest of the crew was split simply between the men (5) and the boys (6).

Rules is rules!

All crew members had to swear to obey strict rules called articles.

- Every man has an equal share of food and drink.
- Gambling for money is forbidden.
- Lights and candles below deck must be out by 8pm.
- Weapons must always be clean and ready for use.
- Musicians may have only one day off a week.
- No women on board.
- Everyone has the right to vote.

Pirates in paradise

Madagascar, in the Indian Ocean, became a pirate 'kingdom' at the end of the 17th century. In 1700 the pirate population on the island was reported to be at least 1,500.

Great shake

Port Royal on the island of Jamaica was the place where pirates went to party! But on 7 June 1692 a massive earthquake shook the town. The tremors set off a huge tidal wave: buildings collapsed and over 2,000 people perished.

PEGLEG

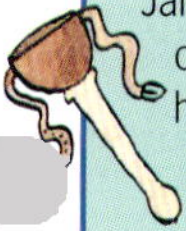

François le Clerc, a 16th-century French privateer, was better known as 'Jambe de Bois' because of his wooden leg. He has hobbled into the history books as the first one-legged pirate.

Caribbean castle

This stronghold on Saint Thomas in the Virgin Islands was the retreat where Blackbeard plotted his ruthless raids. Now (more than 275 years after Blackbeard's death) it is safe for tourists to enter the castle!

Rough Justice

Victims of piracy suffered horribly at the hands of their captors and pirates themselves risked terrible treatment if they broke their own rules. Read on, if you dare.

Marked for life
If pirates captured by the British Navy were not hanged, they were branded with the letter P on the forehead.

Flogging
Minor offences were punishable by flogging. The pirate to be whipped was forced to make his own cat o'nine tails by unravelling rope and knotting the end of each strand.

Walking the plank
Believe it or not, there is just one account of this dastardly deed ever happening.

Keel hauling
A rope was tied to the victim's hands and feet before he was dropped overboard and dragged along the rough underside of the ship. By the time he was pulled up on the other side, he might have drowned. But if he was still alive, his body would be covered in bruises and his skin ripped to shreds.

A gruesome twosome

The infamous Blackbeard was hunted down by a naval officer in 1718. He died in hand-to-hand combat. His severed head was hung from the bowsprit of a British Navy ship.

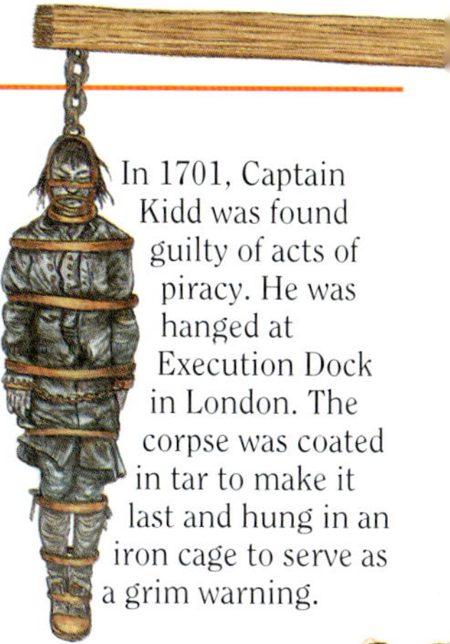

In 1701, Captain Kidd was found guilty of acts of piracy. He was hanged at Execution Dock in London. The corpse was coated in tar to make it last and hung in an iron cage to serve as a grim warning.

Torture

Pirates had a whole catalogue of cruelties that they used if their hostages were reluctant to reveal the whereabouts of concealed valuables. Stretching a victim's limbs with cords while at the same time beating them with sticks was a common torture.

Slashing off ears or fingers could also encourage a quick confession.

More obstinate captives had burning matches placed between their fingers and were gagged to prevent any attempts to blow them out!

One unlucky victim was put in a barrel of gunpowder while a lighted fuse was held to his face.

Marooned

A pirate who deserted ship in battle or was caught stealing from his crew mates would be abandoned on an uninhabited island with just a day's supply of water, a firearm and a ration of gunpowder and shot. The chances of being picked up by a passing ship were remote to say the least.

Deadly Medley

Pirates took no chances when they went into battle. After letting off a barrage of cannon fire, bombs and grenades, they boarded an enemy ship armed to the teeth (or, in some cases, gums). Here are just some of the fearsome firearms and bloody blades you might find in a pirate's arsenal.

Big guns

Working in the gun crew was a dangerous job. Each cannon weighed around two tonnes and was tied to the ship's side by breaching ropes. The violent rebound when the cannon was fired meant the ropes sometimes snapped. So if you weren't deafened by the blasts or blown up by an accidental gunpowder explosion, you might be flattened by an unleashed cannon rolling about the deck.

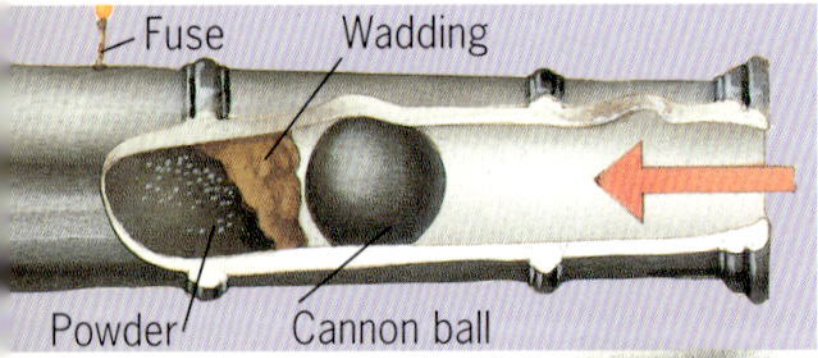

Pirates sometimes fired double, chained cannon balls to cause maximum damage to enemy rigging.

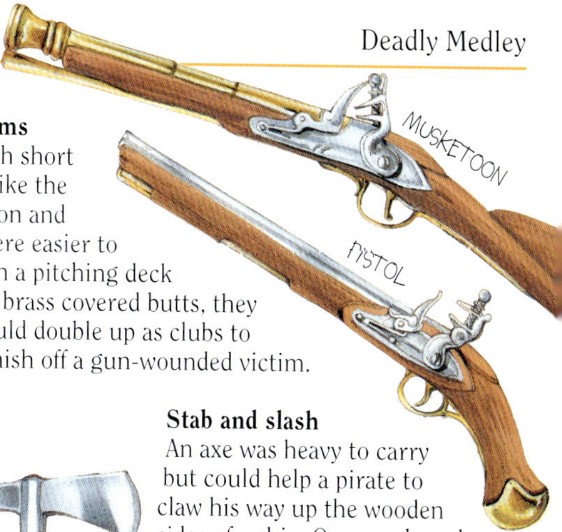

Small arms

Guns with short barrels, like the musketoon and pistol, were easier to handle on a pitching deck and with brass covered butts, they could double up as clubs to finish off a gun-wounded victim.

Stab and slash

An axe was heavy to carry but could help a pirate to claw his way up the wooden sides of a ship. Once on board, the cutlass, with its short, curved blade, was ideal for wielding on a cramped deck. Anything longer would be easily caught up in the rigging. And for combat in the dark below deck, the short dirk could be drawn and used with lethal accuracy.

Home-thrown

Pirates stuffed gunpowder into home-made glass grenades and lobbed them from the bow of the ship. They also used smoke bombs made from a smouldering mixture of tar and rags to cause panic on enemy decks. Spiked crowsfeet would lame and lacerate barefoot sailors.

WATER PISTOLS?

It was a wise precaution to carry several pistols into battle. Not only were they slow to reload, there was always the danger that the gun wouldn't fire at all if the powder was damp or the trigger was rusty!

Battle Tactics

Pirates had lots of horrible ploys up their sleeves to bring them victory over their victims in battle.

Hooked!
If a treasure ship ignored enemy fire and tried to escape from an attack, pirates swung a grappling hook tied to the end of a rope into the rigging.

Dangerous decks
Most crews were overpowered by heavily-armed and battle-crazed pirates. But in 1710 the captain of a small galley covered the decks of his ship with broken bottles when he was attacked by French privateers. The rogues were forced to abandon their attack.

FRIEND OR FOE?

There are reports of pirates boarding enemy ships heavily disguised as ladies in distress. Another of their tricks was to fly a friendly flag and then hoist the dreaded Jolly Roger at the last minute.

Not all at sea

When pirates ran out of food and weapons, a raid on a harbour town was the easiest way to get new supplies. It took a lot of guts for the locals to put up a fight against the raiders.

Canoe cunning

Dugout canoes stolen from local fishermen could be used for sneaking up on an enemy ship. But only the fittest pirates could handle all that paddling!

What a reputation!

It made life much easier if victims would just surrender without a struggle. A violent reputation was usually enough to do the trick.

BATTLE SCARRED

When pirates lost bits of themselves in battle, they were paid compensation: 800 pieces of eight for the loss of a right arm, 400 for other limbs and 100 for an eye or finger.

Prisoners of war

When pirates swarmed aboard a ship they were on the look-out for useful members of the victim crew. A carpenter was worth his weight in gold for his DIY skills. A cooper (who made and mended the barrels for storing food and drink) was also valuable to pirates, as was the ship's surgeon with his medical know-how.

Rich Pickings

Spanish galleons sailed back regularly from the New World laden with fabulous hauls of gold, silver, coins, pearls and jewels. They were sturdily built ships but tricky to steer through heavy seas and no match for the swifter pirate vessels that lay in wait.

SHARING THE SPOILS

On most pirate ships, there were rules for dividing up the plunder. Usually, it was six shares for the captain, two for the master's mate, one for each man in the crew and half a share to each boy.

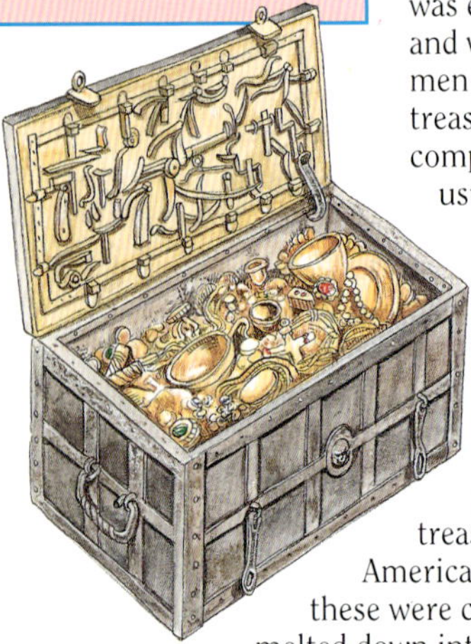

Locked-up loot
A treasure chest full of gold was every pirate's dream and would have needed four men just to lift it! A Spanish treasure chest had a very complex set of locks and usually had a false keyhole on the front (the real one would be hidden somewhere else).

Making a mint
Spanish colonists pillaged gold and silver treasures from South America. More often than not, these were chucked into a furnace, melted down into bars, crudely sliced into coins and hastily stamped with the royal arms of Spain before being shipped back to the Spanish treasury. Sixteen silver pieces of eight were worth one gold doubloon.

All that glitters is not gold
Of course it was always nice to come away from a raid with untold riches, but pirates weren't fussy. They'd carry off weapons, ammunition, food, barrels of rum, or even rope, sails and tools. And a real find would be the ship's medicine chest.

Booby booty
Sometimes pirates would swarm aboard a ship, only to find its hold empty or full of a bulky cargo that they would be unable to pilfer with the necessary speed.

Buried treasure?
Most pirates preferred to squander their plunder as soon as they returned to port. Blackbeard is said to have once buried treasure on a desert island, leaving one of his 14 wives there to guard it.

Lost and found
1 Sam Bellamy and his pirate crew captured the *Whydah* in 1717. But the ship was caught in a fierce storm and struck the rocks off Cape Cod. Only two of the 146 men survived. In 1984, the wreck of the *Whydah* was discovered and over 8,000 coins have been salvaged at a cost of US $6 million.
2 Henry Morgan's flagship blew up and sank with its treasure in the Caribbean in 1669.
3 A ship called *Rosario* was ambushed by English pirates and set adrift in 1681 as they supposed its cargo to be tin when in fact it was laden with silver.

Rogues' Gallery

Step inside this hall of infamy and come face to face with some of the most notorious pirate legends.

Blackbeard

Born Edward Teach in 1680, Blackbeard earned his nickname from his wild and terrifying appearance. When he went into battle, he twisted burning fuses into his long black hair and beard so that he appeared in a cloud of dense smoke.

Henry Morgan

Morgan ran away to sea as a boy and embarked on a successful pirate career. His daring privateer attacks on Spanish galleons won him a knighthood from King Charles II of England. When he died in 1688, Morgan was deputy governor of Jamaica.

Dragut Reis

After serving as a galley slave, Dragut Reis escaped his Christian captors and became a ruthless corsair commander. From 1547 he led many bloody attacks on Christian ports. He was killed in action, besieging the island of Malta in 1565.

William Kidd

Born in Scotland in 1645, William Kidd was a rich New York businessman when he was hired as a pirate-catcher. But, after murdering one of his crew in a fit of temper, he turned outlaw and committed several acts of piracy.

Henry Avery

Avery seized control of a privateering vessel in 1694. After ambushing an Indian treasure ship, each man in his crew received loot worth over £2,000. But Avery was swindled out of most of his fortune and died in poverty.

Bartholomew Roberts

Unusually for a pirate captain, Roberts was teetotal. He banned gambling on his ships. At the height of his career in 1721, he had a squadron of four vessels with a total crew of 508 men.

Chui Apoo

This Hong Kong barber (would you let him cut *your* hair?) turned to piracy in 1845. He controlled a vast fleet in the South China Sea.

Pirates in Petticoats

Going to sea wasn't all a man's game. Here are the ladies who found their sea legs and put the 'lass' into cutlass!

Double trouble
Mary Read ran away from home at the age of 14, dressed as a boy. After a spell fighting in the army, she embarked on a ship bound for the Caribbean. It was while she was serving under the command of 'Calico' Jack Rackham that Read met his pirate wife, Anne Bonny.

Courtroom drama
In 1720 Bonny and Read were put on trial with the rest of Rackham's crew. The women were spared when they both announced that they were pregnant.

Calico Jack
Calico Jack was so called because he wore bright cotton outfits that made him stand out in a crowd.

Maid of honour
There were women pirate catchers too. Ann Mills fought bravely in the British Navy when it was stamping out piracy in the Far East.

PIRATE QUEENS

- Alwilda was the daughter of a Scandinavian king in the 5th century. She didn't fancy the prospect of an arranged marriage to Prince Alf of Denmark, so she ran away to sea and captained an all-male pirate crew. When Alf was sent to hunt her down, Alwilda was so impressed by his fighting skills that the pair got married!

- Lai Choi San ran a fleet of pirate junks in the 1920s and was known as the 'Queen of the Macao pirates'. This pint-sized woman was a ruthless leader and even killed her own husband.

'Have you met the wife?'

Ching Shih married the pirate leader Cheng I in 1801. When her husband died in 1807 she was left in charge of 1,800 ships and 8,000 men. She paid a reward for every severed head brought back after an attack.

Wine, women and song

Women pirates may have been in the minority, but what about pirates' women? A survey of American pirates active between 1716 and 1726 shows that only 23 out of 521 were married. But many an off-duty rogue enjoyed the company of women!

Fantasy...

Did you know that even Tintin, the comic-strip hero, has to pit his wits against a cunning pirate captain called Red Rackham? Pirates make great 'baddies' in any plot, here are just a few.

LONG JOHN SILVER

From Long John Silver...
In 1883 Robert Louis Stevenson created Long John Silver, the most famous fictional one-legged sea robber. He staggers and swaggers his way through the classic novel, *Treasure Island*.

... to the silver screen
In the 1940s pirate movies were all the rage. But the pirates were romantic heroes rather than villains. They were always squeaky-clean and a far cry from the scurvy-ridden rascals of reality.

ERROL FLYNN

HOLLYWOOD HOOK

Peter Pan, published in 1904, tells the adventures of Peter and Wendy and their brave struggles against Captain Hook and his motley crew. Steven Spielberg turned the book into a box office hit.

DUSTIN HOFFMAN AS HOOK

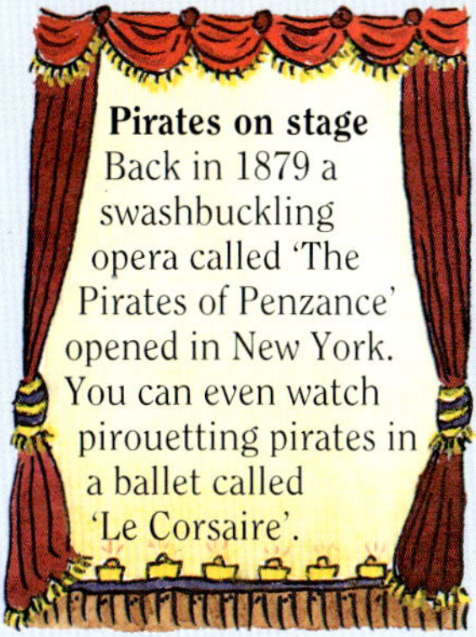

Pirates on stage
Back in 1879 a swashbuckling opera called 'The Pirates of Penzance' opened in New York. You can even watch pirouetting pirates in a ballet called 'Le Corsaire'.

FACT OR FICTION?

You shouldn't believe all the stories you read about real-life pirates.
Did Captain Kidd really bury his Bible in a defiant gesture when he turned outlaw? Did Blackbeard's headless corpse swim around the ship where he had fought to the death?

...or Reality?

The last buccaneers were rounded up by the British Navy in the 18th century. The French invaded Algiers in 1830 and put an end to corsair activity in the Mediterranean. And in the Far East, the great pirate fleets were destroyed in 1849. But if you thought piracy belongs to the history books, think again. The days of plunder are back. Worldwide, there were 170 reported pirate attacks in 1995. Modern pirates are high-tech: they are armed with Kalashnikov rifles and make their getaway after a raid in powerful motorboats.

1990s PIRATES

INDEX

Written by Helen Torimmer
Designed by Brian Robins and Jacqueline Palmer

First published in 1996 by HarperCollins Children's Books, A Division of HarperCollins Publishers Ltd, 77–85 Fulham Palace Road, London W6 8JB

ISBN: 0 00 197961 2

Illustrations: Susanna Addario, Douglas Hall, Charlotte Hard, Kevin Maddison, Claudia Saraceni, Thomas Trojer

Photographs: British Museum 2, 24b; Eye Ubiquitous/ © B.P. Adams 17; Mary Evans Picture Library 24t, 30t; National Maritime Museum Picture Library 4, 6, 7, 9, 12, 28; National Portrait Gallery 8; Ronald Grant Archive 30c, 30b; Sygma/ © E. Pasquier 31.

A CIP record for this book is available from the British Library

Printed and bound in Hong Kong